Rags and Tatters from the
Far North of Japan

つぎ、はぎ、いかす。青森のぼろ布文化

小出由紀子、都築響一

アスペクト

そんなに昔のことじゃない、たった数十年前まで、貧しい農村といえば、人はまず東北をイメージした。本州のどん詰まり、東北の端っこの青森県で極貧の生活にあえいできた農民が生み出した、恐るべきテキスタイルの美学、それが"ぼろ"である。

民芸に詳しい人ならば、青森というと津軽のこぎん刺しや、南部の菱刺しを思い浮かべるだろう。雪国の女性たちによって伝えられてきたこぎんや菱刺しは、昭和初期の民芸運動に発見されて、一躍脚光を浴びるようになった。もっともっと肌に近いところで農民の日常のなかに生きてきた"ぼろ"は、いまだに顧みられることもなく、「貧しい東北を象徴するもの」として、恥ずかしさとともに葬り去られようとしている。

寒冷地である青森では綿花の栽培ができず（綿花の育つ北限は福島県あたりといわれている）、農漁民の日常衣料は麻を栽培して織った麻布だった。現在の青森県は江戸時代、津軽藩領と南部藩領に二分されていたが、どちらの藩において絹織物は一部特権階級のものだったし、寒冷地であるにもかかわらず（青森市は全国の県庁所在地のうちで、もっとも積雪量の多い都市である）、藩政時代を通じて農民が木綿を着用することを禁じていた。したがって田畑での作業着から、赤ん坊のおしめ、長い冬の夜を過ごす布団まで、農民の身につけるものはすべて、麻布のみで賄う時代が長く続いたのである。1枚の麻布で寒すぎれば、何枚でも重ねていく。枚数を重ねれば防寒性が増すし、糸を刺していけば丈夫になる。傷んで穴が空けば小布でつくろい、また布と布のあいだに麻屑を入れて温かくする。そうした厳しい生活環境から生まれたサバイバルのかたち、それがこぎんであり菱刺しであり、ぼろなのだ。

江戸時代に関東、近畿では農民の常用着として普及していた木綿が、本格的に東北地方に行きわたるようになったのは、明治24年の東北本線開通後だといわれる。沿線から離れた寒村では、普及はさらに遅れただろう。

肌に優しい木綿の反物はもちろん、麻の古布からぼろ切れにいたるまで、当時の貧しい人々にとって、あらゆる布はたいへんな貴重品だった。どんなに小さな布切れでも大事に取っておいて、

つぎ、はぎ、いかす。青森のぼろ布文化
小出由紀子・都築響一

それが風呂敷包みひとつになるくらい溜まったら、それだけ持って女は嫁に行く——そんなことが珍しくなかったという。

　着古した衣は米のとぎ汁に浸して縫い糸を引き抜き、小布1枚、糸1本にいたるまで粗末にすることなく、すり切れた衣服や布団に縫い重ねていく。あるいは数ミリの細さまで裂いて、それを麻糸とともに織ってサキオリ（裂織）と呼ばれる、独特の風合いを持つ布によみがえらせる。最終的に、どうしようもなく使い切った布切れは、縄に編んで、農作業のときに頭に巻きつける。端に火をつければ少しずつ燃えて、かっこうの蚊除けになるのだという。大地から生まれた麻が布になって、ぼろになって、また灰になって大地に還っていく。

　リサイクルという言葉すら白々しく思えるほどの、布への愛着とともに生きてきた人々がいて、それがいま、きれいさっぱり忘れ去られようとしている。青森県内に数多い美術館・博物館で、こぎんや菱刺しを観賞することはできても、ぼろは1枚も見ることができないのだ。

　ここに紹介するのは東北地方でほとんどただひとり、昭和40年代から青森県内の山・農・漁村を歩き回り、"ぼろ"とひとまとめに呼ばれる、布と人との愛のあかしを探し求め、保存してきた田中忠三郎さんのコレクションである。

　そっくり復刻して、フランス語かイタリア語のタグと高い値段をつければ、そのままハイファッションになるにちがいない、完璧な完成度。それが民芸や現代のキルト、パッチワーク作家のように、きれいなものを作りたくて作ったのではなくて、そのときあるものをなんでもいいから重ねていって、少しでも温かく、丈夫にしたいという切実な欲求だけから生まれた、その純度。

　優れたアウトサイダー・アートが職業現代美術作家に与えるショックのように、雪国の貧農が生んだ"ぼろ"の思いがけない美の世界は、ファッション・デザインに関わるすべての人間に根源的な問いを突きつけ、目を背けることを許さない。

青森県

Only a few decades ago, Tohoku "snow country"– and especially Aomori Prefecture – was synonymous to most Japanese with dire poverty. Situated dead-end on the northernmost tip of the main island of Honshu, Aomori was home to dirt poor farmers who, out of desperate necessity, created an astonishing textile aesthetic out of *boro* – mere "rags."

To those familiar with mingei and the Japan Folk Craft Movement, Aomori typically suggests intricate *kogin-sashi* and *hishi-zashi* geometric needlework "discovered" in the region during the pre-war years. Much closer to the lives of the people, however, boro stitchery remains largely unknown, even intentionally buried as an embarrassing reminder of "the poverty that was Tohoku."

The frozen north was too cold to grow cotton – the northernmost limit for cultivating cotton is Fukushima Prefecture, over 300 kms to the south – so the local folk grew and wove hemp for clothing. Throughout the Edo Period (1600-1868), when silk was restricted to a privileged handful of samurai class families, commoners were also forbidden to wear cotton despite the bitter climate (Aomori City has the highest snowfall of any prefectural capital in the whole of Japan.) Thus everything from work clothes to babies diapers to futon bedding for the long winter nights was sewn from stiff, scratchy hemp cloth. And if a single layer wasn't warm enough, they stitched and reinforced layer on layer, patching holes and stuffing hemp fuzz in between for whatever little insulation they could get. Boro was the shape of survival in this inhospitable land.

Throughout this same Edo Period, farmers down in the Kanto plains around what is now Tokyo and the Kinki region further southwest toward Kyoto and Osaka wore cotton. It wasn't until 1892, when the first Tohoku Railway line was opened, that anything cotton really found its way north, and even then it didn't reach isolated mountain villages until much later.

Not just rolls of soft cotton yardage, but any scraps of old cloth were coveted commodities to the poor folk of Tohoku. The tiniest

Boro: Rags and Tatters from the Far North of Japan

Yukiko Koide & Kyoichi Tsuzuki

precious snippets were saved. A lowly furoshiki wrap-cloth filled with threadbare shreds and tatters was all a girl took with her when she got married.

They soaked worn-out old clothes in rice-rinsing water in order to loosen and pull out threads, never wasting the least scrap, stitching over ripped and ragged layers as thick as they could. Or else, they cut it into thin ribbons, which they re-loomed with hemp warps into distinctive nubby *saki-ori* – literally "tear-woven" – cloth. And as a last resort, any remaining bits of fiber were braided into rope to be worn as headbands while doing farm work. They say these ropes also burned very slowly, making them useful for repelling mosquitos. Hemp from the land makes cloth,

becomes rags and finally turns to ash and returns to the soil.

Long before "recycling" was drummed into our heads, here were people whose loving frugality toward cloth was a genuine engrained in their lives – yet total forgotten today. The museums of Aomori are filled with fine examples of *kogin-sashi* and *hishi-zashi* stitchery, but not a single piece of real boro.

Presented herein is the collection of one Chuzaburo Tanaka who, virtually alone in all of Tohoku, walked the farming and fishing villages of Aomori from the mid-1960s, searching out these traces of the locals' love of fabric known as boro.

If exactingly reproduced and labeled with French or Italian designer tags, these "not-so-glad rags" would undoubtedly fetch high-end prices, so perfectly artless is their detailing. Not that they're in any way "precious" like *mingei* "folk craft" or contemporary auteur patchwork quilts; no, these are products, pure and simple, of a shivering desire to thickly overlay whatever was on hand for heavy-duty warmth.

Just as consummate "outsider art" shocked contemporary art professionals, the beauty and sheer compositional skill of these boro creations made by impoverished country folk pose fundamental questions to fashion and design circles everywhere.

Aomori

ドンジャ

185 × 150 cm

南部地方の農山村では、冬の夜、家族は裸で、これを被って眠った。麻布に、縞や型染めなどさまざまな古手木綿の布や手拭を重ねて縫ってある。中には麻屑が入っていて、重さ14キロ。ひとりでは持てないほど重い。

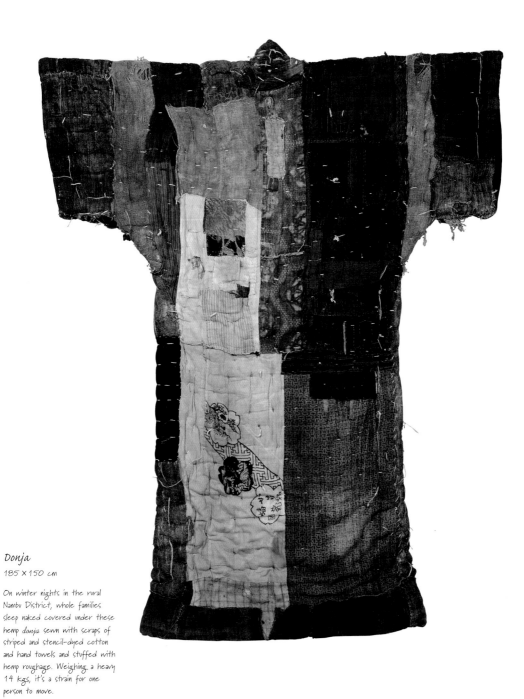

Donja
185 × 150 cm

On winter nights in the rural
Nambu District, whole families
sleep naked covered under these
hemp *donja* sewn with scraps of
striped and stencil-dyed cotton
and hand towels and stuffed with
hemp roughage. Weighing a heavy
14 kgs, it's a strain for one
person to move.

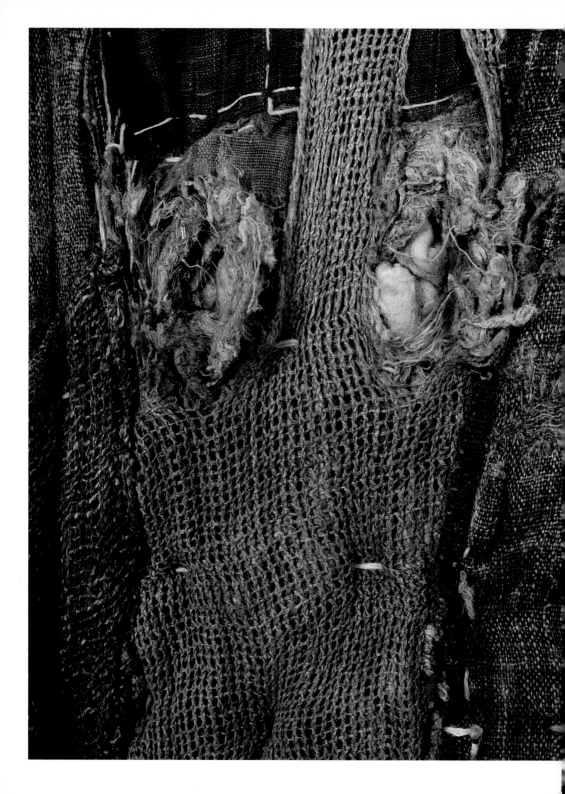

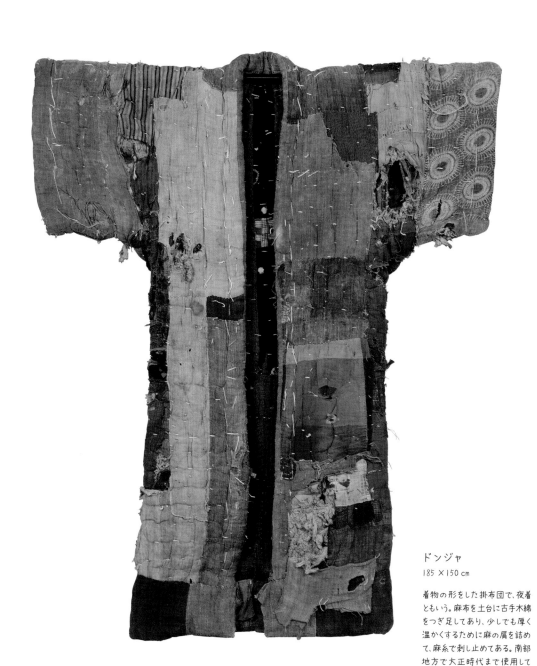

ドンジャ

185 × 150 cm

着物の形をした掛布団で、夜着
ともいう。麻布を土台に古手木綿
をつぎ足してあり、少しでも厚く
温かくするために麻の屑を詰め
て、麻糸で刺し止めてある。南部
地方で大正時代まで使用して
いたもの。

Donja

185 x 150 cm

This kimono-shaped combination
quilt and night-robe of hemp cloth
patched with old pieces of cotton
was stuffed with hemp refuse for
every extra increment of warmth
and stitched up with hemp
thread. Used in the Nambu
District until the Taisho Era
(1911–1925).

ドンジャ
148 × 122 cm

着古して薄くなった麻の野良着を
10枚以上重ねてある。木綿の布
や綿(わた)の入手が困難だった南部
地方の人々の知恵が生んだ冬の
寝具。浅葱(あさぎ)色や紺色に染めた
麻布の年月を経た表情が美しい。

Donja
148 × 122 cm

Layered together out of ten old
farming kimono, this winter
bedding attests to the practical
wisdom Nambu villagers who had no
access to cotton cloth or
wadding. The light and deep
indigo-dyed hemp cloth has aged
beautifully.

着せて、食わせて

「泣いてあやぐる形見分け」――田中忠三郎さんから伺った、津軽の諺は衝撃的だった。肉親が亡くなると、遺族がその着物を泣きながら取りあうというのだ。現代であればさしずめ預金や証券、不動産の奪いあいといったところだが、第二次世界大戦後になるまで、青森では衣服は金銭同様に大切なものだった。

本州の最北端に位置する青森は三方を海に囲まれ、自然豊かな土地である。しかし冬の寒さは過酷で、着ることは食べることと同じくらい死活問題だった。

家族に衣服を用意し管理することを、青森では〈センタク〉と言い、主婦の仕事だった。農家の女性たちは農作業や家事、育児に加えて、麻を栽培し、刈り取り、加工し、糸を績み、繕り、布に織りあげた。たいへんな手間と時間をかけて得た布はすべて――小さな布の切れはしや、糸屑さえも――大事な財産だった。

ひとりのおばあさんが遺した風呂敷包みの中を見せていただいたとき、言葉を失った。数百枚もの木綿の布切れが包まれていた。不揃いの小布は洗ってアイロンがあてられ、色別に整理されていた。いつか使おうと思って、大切にとっておいたものだという。驚いたのは、これだけのつぎ布を持てたのは資産家だけだったということだ。貧しい人は小布さえ持てず、親戚や裕福な家に布をもらいに行かなければならなかった。

物が溢れ、使い捨ての時代に慣れてしまった私たちには、この風呂敷包みは、貧しさの名残にしか見えないかもしれない。けれど、物質的な豊かさとひきかえに私たちは大切なものを見失ってしまったのではないだろうか。困窮生活の中で、物を作り、いとおしみ、使い切る充足感――それは、人間の命についても言えることではないだろうか。

Feeding and clothing

" Tears and bickering over keepsakes" – a graphic saying from Tsugaru, which according to Chuzaburo Tanaka fairy accurately describes funerals in Aomori in the old days: when someone died, the relations all cried as they fought over the who got the kimono. Nowadays the bickering is over savings and securities and property, but up until right after World War II clothing was just as valuable as money in Aomori.

Situated at the northernmost tip of Honshu with the sea on three sides. Aomori is rich in natural beauty but bitter cold in winter. Clothing, like food, is a matter of life and death.

In Aomori, doing the "laundry" – meaning providing and minding the family's clothes – was women's work. In addition to farming, household chores and raising children, farmwomen grew, harvested and processed hemp, then spun and wove it into cloth. The product of such intensive labor, every little bit of cloth – cuttings and wastage included – was precious.

Tanaka showed me the contents of an old lady's *furoshiki* wrap-cloth: hundreds of irregular cotton scraps, each washed, color sorted and ironed, all carefully saved up to be used who-knows-when. I was at a loss for words. This many swatches, he said, made her a rich woman! Poor folk were those who had to beg their rich relations for bits of cloth.

Accustomed as we are to the "convenience age" of one-time use commodities, that parcel of scraps may have seemed a sad reminder by-gone poverty, but conversely hasn't the very abundance of things today made us lose sight of something more important? Wasn't life more alive when people met difficulties by making, caring for and using every last speck of their necessities?

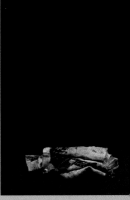

丹前
132 × 122 cm

冬に室内で着る防寒着。寒冷地
の青森では綿花の栽培ができ
なかったため、織物になる前の
糸も綿も貴重品だった。古手木
綿の小布をつなぎ合わせて
作った丹前の中には、綿が少しと
麻の小布がたくさん入っている。

Tanzen
132 × 122 cm

Thick home-wear for winter.
Even cotton thread wadding was
a rarity in the frozen northlands
of Aomori, so this patched cotton
rag *tanzen* is filled mostly with
hemp cloth scraps.

丹前
133 × 130 cm

冬に室内で着る防寒着。明治24年
東北本線開通後、東北地方にも
木綿製品が流通するようになっ
たが、農山村では貴重品だった。
麻屑を詰めたドンジャは姿を消
したが、この丹前には綿が少しと
麻布が入っている。

Tanzen
133 × 130 cm

Thick home-wear for winter.
With the opening of the Tohoku
Railway in 1892, a precious few
cotton products finally began to
reach Tohoku. The hemp
waste-stuffed *donja* faded away,
but *tanzen* like this still only had
a meager ratio of cotton to hemp
cloth inside.

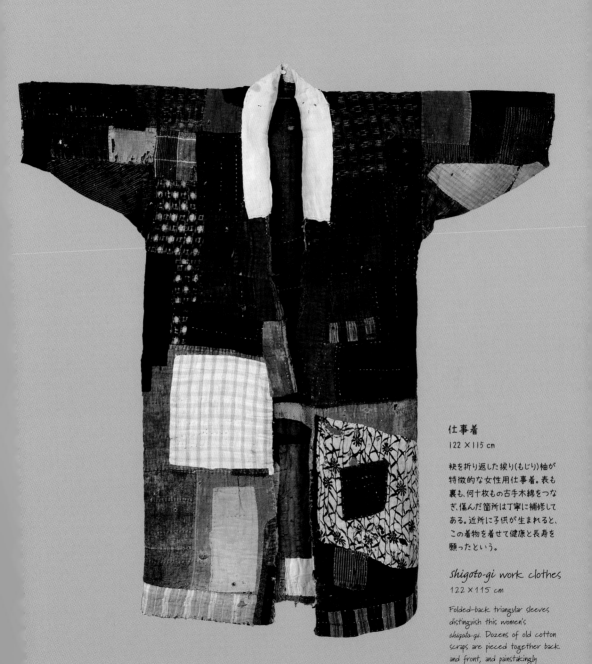

仕事着
122 × 115 cm

袂を折り返した捩り（もじり）袖が
特徴的な女性用仕事着。表も
裏も、何十枚もの古手木綿をつな
ぎ、傷んだ箇所は丁寧に補修して
ある。近所に子供が生まれると、
この着物を着せて健康と長寿を
願ったという。

shigoto-gi work clothes
122 × 115 cm

Folded-back triangular sleeves
distinguish this women's
shigoto-gi. Dozens of old cotton
scraps are pieced together back
and front, and painstakingly
mended where worn. Newborn
babies in the neighborhood were
swaddled in such clothes to wish
them health and long life.

袖無し
98 × 64 cm

麻布の着物が古くなり、袖を取って
ベストにしたもの。新しい木綿の
反物や着物を買えなかった人々
は、古手木綿の小布を買い求め、
昔からあった麻の着物につぎ足
した。モダンな構成がまるで抽
象絵画のようだ。

sodenashi
98 × 64 cm

A sleeveless vest made out of an
old hemp kimono. Those who
couldn't afford new cotton
kimono or fabric, bought assorted
old cotton scraps and simply
patched up their old hemp kimono.
The bold composition is something
out of an abstract painting.

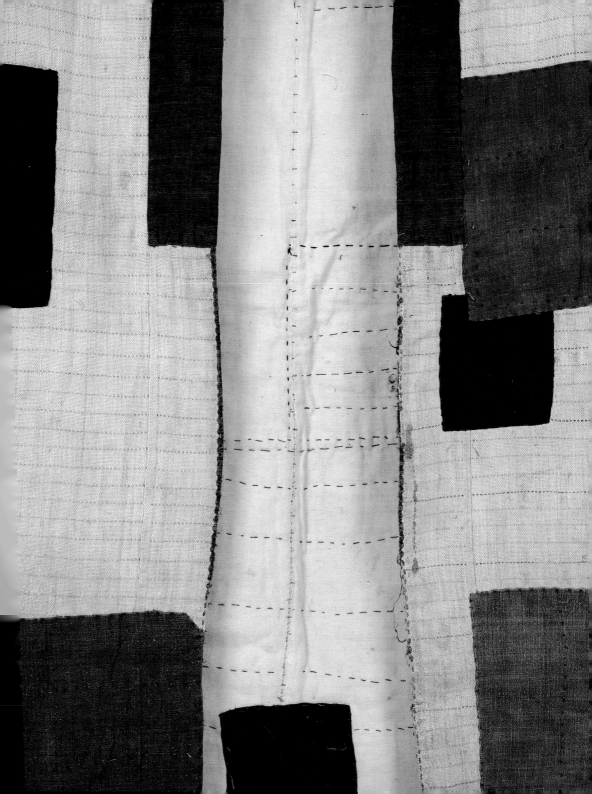

仕事着
135 × 132 cm

サグリ、サッコリなどと呼ばれる、
漁師や船乗りの仕事着。日本海
交易により、古手木綿が流通す
るようになると、それを細く引き
裂き緯糸として織った。経糸は
麻。防水・防寒に優れ、日本海
沿岸で広く用いられた。

shigoto-gi work clothes
135 × 132 cm

Also called *saguri* or *sakkori*,
fishermen or seamen's *shigoto-gi*
like this were warm and fairly
water-repellent. Woven of
sea-trade cotton rags thinly
slivered into wefts with hemp
warps, they were widely worn
along the coast.

限られた素材：麻

　日本国内で綿花の栽培が行なわれるようになったのは 16 世紀後半、木綿の衣服が普及したのは江戸時代だった。それ以前、庶民の衣服は、大麻、苧麻、おひょう、科（しな）、藤、楮（こうぞ）など、樹や草の繊維を織った布で作られていた。地域によって違いはあるものの、これらの植物繊維を織った布をサグリ、サッコリ、サックリなどと呼ぶのは、靭皮を「裂く」行為に由来するようだ。

　なかでも栽培ができて、採取や加工が比較的楽な麻は古くから、日本全国で広く使われた。青森も例外ではなく、縄文時代の三内丸山遺跡から、麻の種が見つかっている。

　麻布は撥水性がよく、織り目が粗い。夏場に着るには風通しがよくて涼しいが、冬場には寒い。そこで青森の女性たちは、麻布を2枚、3枚合わせ、刺子をほどこして着物に仕立てた。布の耐久性と保温性を高めるための、実用の手技である。

　青森といえば、津軽地方のこぎん刺しと南部地方の菱刺しが有名だが、これももとはといえば、紺色や浅葱色に染めた麻布の目を綿糸でふさいで防寒性を高め、布の耐久性を向上させる機能がおしゃれへと発展したものだ。これらの可憐な手仕事を育んだ女性たちの技術や美的感覚は、普段着や仕事着にも惜しみなく発揮されている。装飾性を省いたシンプルな縦刺しや横刺しであるが、ディテールに目を凝らして欲しい。緻密な刺し目や、身体を保護しつつも、その中で身体を動かしやすい、刺子の糸のほどよい張り具合などは熟練した技術の証である。

　その寡黙な美しさから、厳しい生活に鍛錬された人間のつつましい佇まいが見えてくる。

kogin-sashi and *hishi-zashi* needlework of the
Tsugaru and Nambu districts respectively,

肌着シャツ
71 × 130 cm

青森の冬は長く、厳しい。木綿、
毛織物、絹など、ありとあらゆる
古布を重ねて、寄せ縫いした肌着
は身体にぴったりフィットして温
かく、お年寄りはこれを麻や木
綿の着物の下に着た。

Hadagi undershirt
71 × 130 cm

Winter in Aomori is long and
bitter cold. Cotton, wool, silk,
whatever fabric scraps were to
be had were hobbled together to
make tight-fitting undergarments.
An old person would have worn
this under a hemp or cotton
kimono.

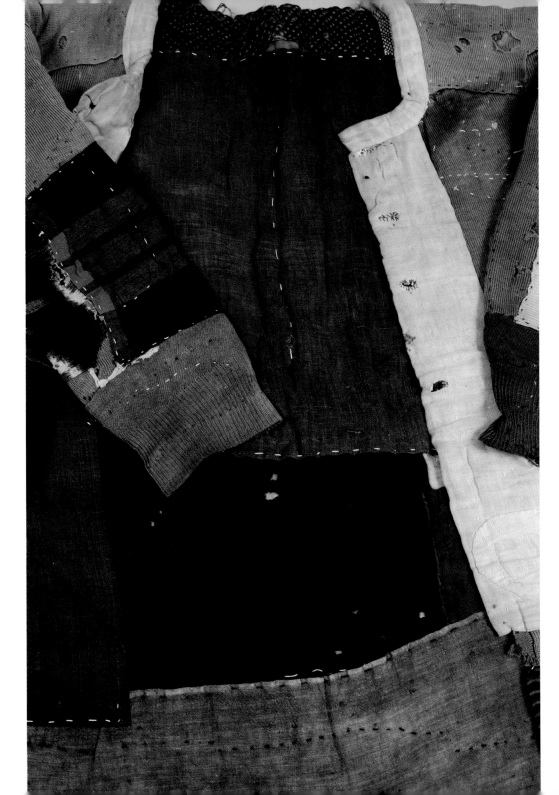

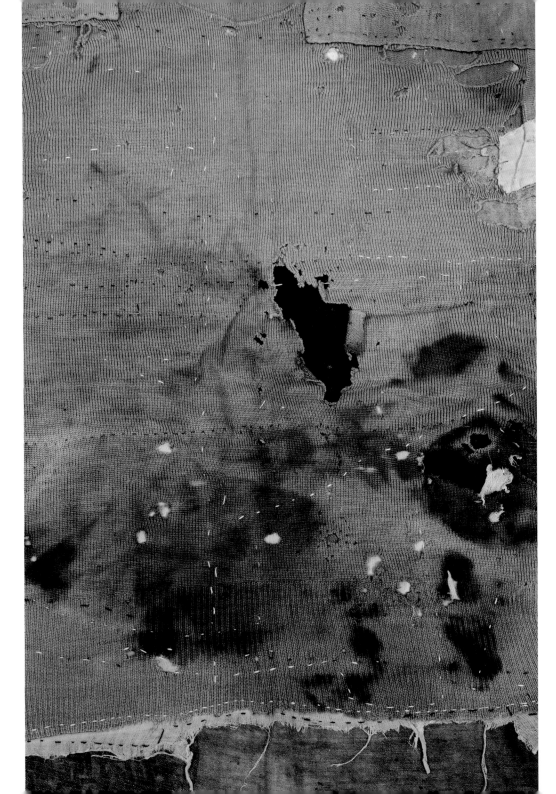

肌着シャツ
71 × 136 cm

大正時代になると、毛織物も
流通し始めた。町の資産家は、
着物の下にメリヤス(伸縮性の
ある毛織物)の肌着を着ること
ができたが、農山村では古着を
工夫してシャツを作り、冬の寒さ
をしのいだ。

Hadagi undershirt
71 × 136 cm

Came the Taisho Era
(1911-1925), trade in wool
began. Well-to-do townsfolk
might wear stretchy woolen
meriyasu under their kimono, but
poor villagers still shivered in
undershirts pieced together out
of old rags.

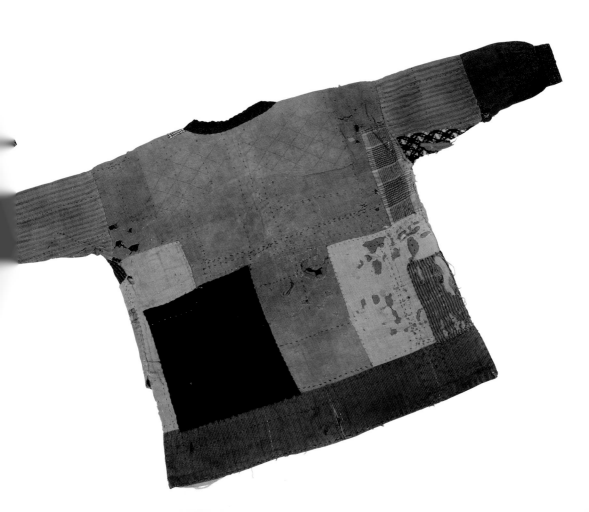

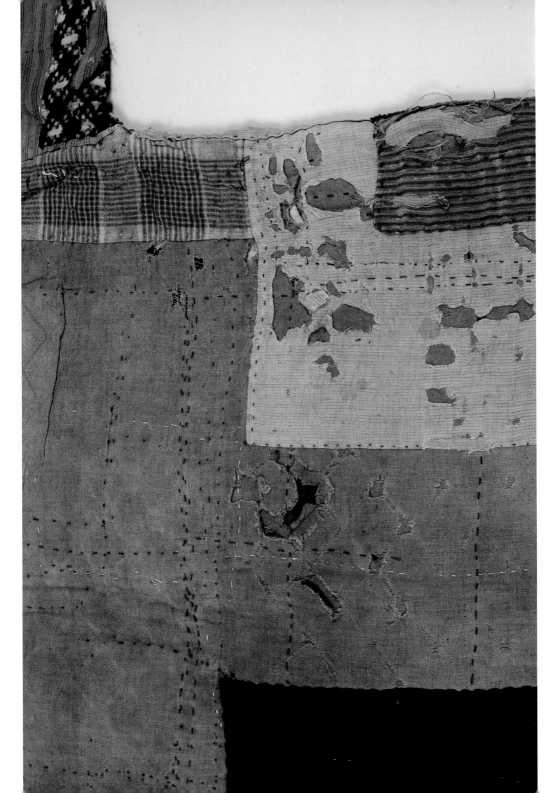

肌着シャツ
78 × 135 cm

メリヤスの肌着は温かく、伸縮
性があり、肌に優しかった。新品
を買えない人々は、古着や古布
をつないでシャツを手作りした。
布の間に綿が詰めてある。

Hadagi undershirt
78 × 135 cm

Stretchy meriyasu undergarments
were warm and soft on the skin.
Those who couldn't afford new
goods made their own undershirts
by hand out of old kimono and
rags, with cotton wadding
stuffed between the cloth.

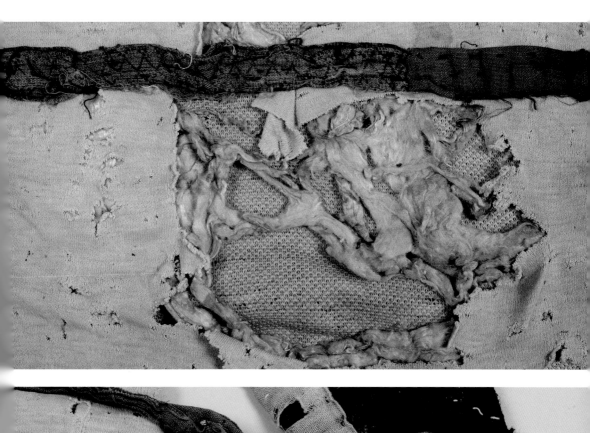

上着
76 × 154 cm

毛織物の上着をつくろって
着続けた。

Jacket
76 × 154 cm

Constant mending kept this wool
coat wearable for decades.

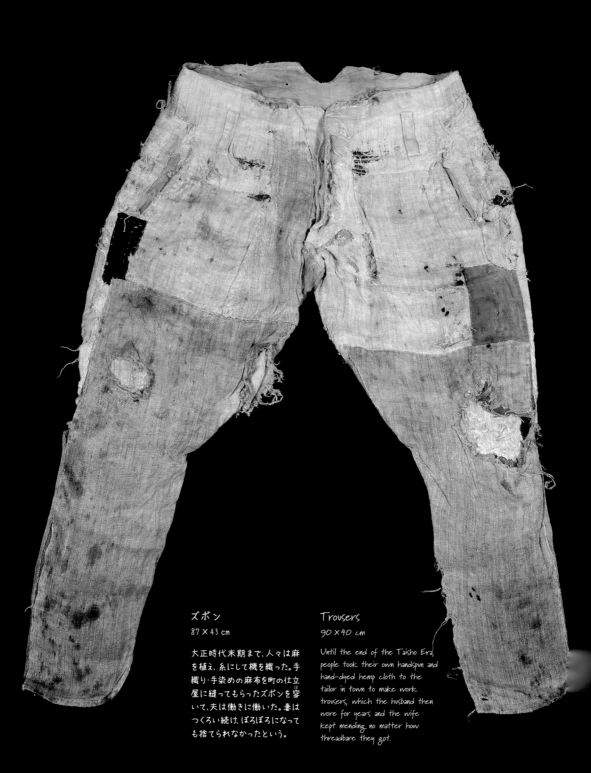

ズボン

87 × 43 cm

大正時代末期まで、人々は麻
を植え、糸にして機を織った。手
織り・手染めの麻布を町の仕立
屋に縫ってもらったズボンを穿
いて、夫は働きに働いた。妻は
つくろい続け、ぼろぼろになって
も捨てられなかったという。

Trousers

90 × 40 cm

Until the end of the Taisho Era,
people took their own handspun and
hand-dyed hemp cloth to the
tailor in town to make work
trousers, which the husband then
wore for years and the wife
kept mending, no matter how
threadbare they got.

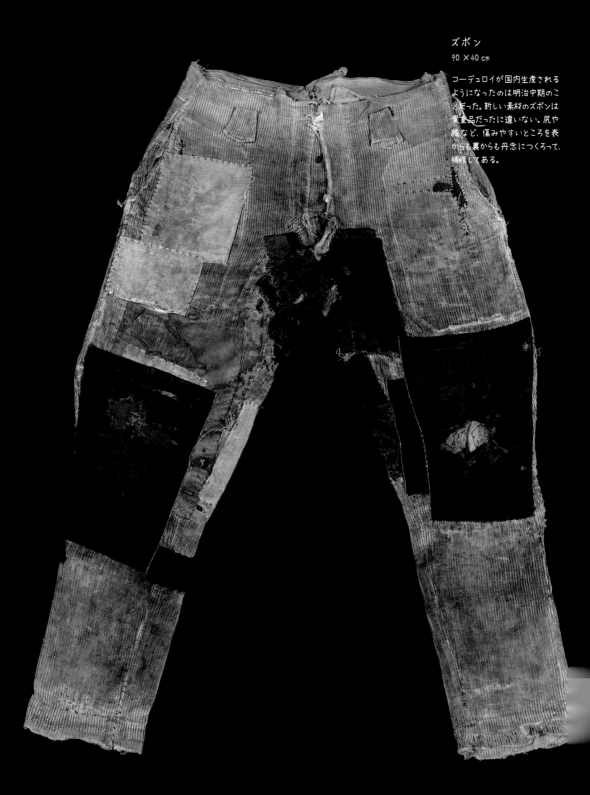

ズボン

90 × 40 cm

コーデュロイが国内生産される
ようになったのは明治中期のこ
とだった。新しい素材のズボンは
貴重品だったに違いない。尻や
膝など、傷みやすいところを表
からも裏からも丹念につくろって、
補修してある。

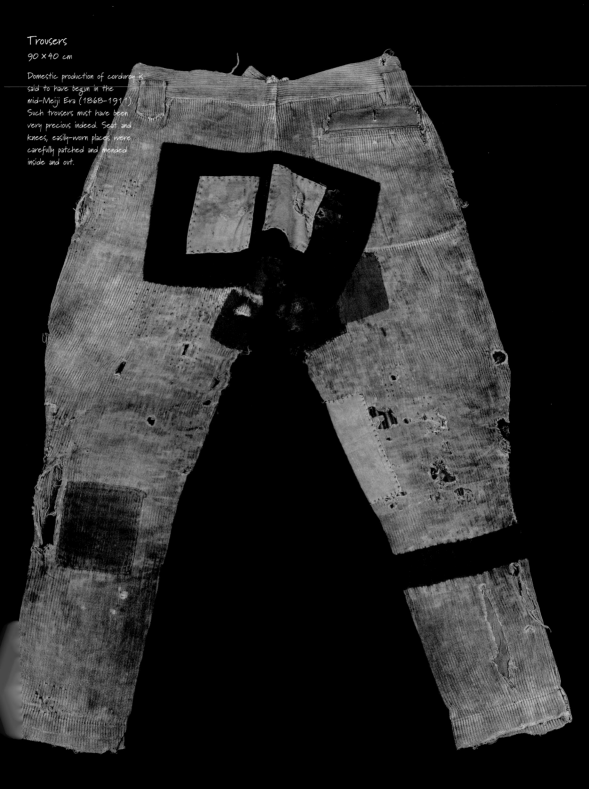

Trousers

90 x 40 cm

Domestic production of corduroy is
said to have begun in the
mid-Meiji Era (1868-1911).
Such trousers must have been
very precious indeed. Seat and
knees, easily-worn places, were
carefully patched and mended
inside and out.

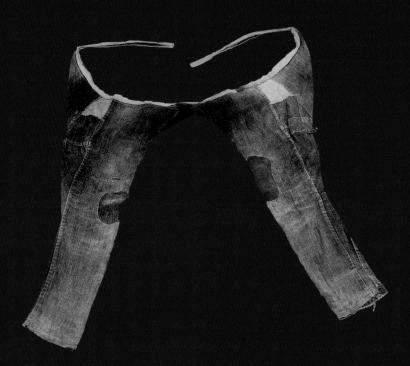

股われ（男性用股引）
89 × 110 cm

ミジカと呼ばれた上着の下に
履いた麻の仕事着。下に木綿の
褌をつけた。麻布を藍で染める
と布が丈夫になり、虫がつかない
と言われ、女たちは手織りの麻布
を染め、男たちは藍染めの上下
を着て野良仕事をした。

Mataware leggings
89 × 110 cm

Under a *mijika* short jacket,
these hemp leggings were worn
over a *fundoshi* crotch strap.
Indigo dyeing was said to make
the hemp cloth strong, and insect
repellent. Women did the weaving
and dyeing, so men could wear
indigo top and bottom when
working in the fields.

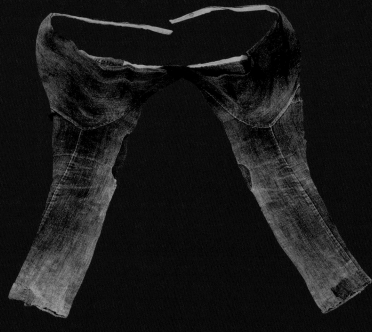

股われ（男性用股引）
95 × 112 cm

ミジカと呼ばれた上着の下に
履いた麻の仕着。下に木綿の
褌をつけた。動きやすいように
裁断を工夫し、破れにくいように
綿密に縫ってある。硬い麻布が
柔らかくなるほど使い込まれて
いるが、ほころびは1つもない。

Mataware leggings
95 × 112 cm

Worn under a *mijika* short
jacket, these hemp leggings
were cleverly patterned and
exactly sewn to prevent
splitting. Worn over a cotton
fundoshi crotch strap with a
drawstring waist, the stiff hemp
cloth has worn pliant, yet there's
not a single split seam.

もんぺ
80 × 40 cm

さまざまな木綿布をつなぎ合わ
せたもんぺは、女性用の仕事着。
紺無地に絣や縞木綿をランダ
ムにつなぎ合わせたデザインに
は、現代のパッチワークに通じる
楽しさがある。

Mompe bloomers
80 × 40 cm

These mompe women's work
wear were pieced together out
of all sorts of cotton cloth.
Random patches of ikat and
striped cotton on an indigo ground
makes a pleasantly contemporary
design.

限られた素材：木綿

　関西や九州など、温暖な地方で生産された木綿を東北地方に伝えたのは北前船の船乗りたちだったという。船員たちが着ていた木綿の仕事着は、麻布衣に比べて肌触りが良いうえに格段に温かく、北国の人々をとりこにした。しかし寒冷地の青森では綿花の栽培ができなかったため、人々は麻布衣に頼り続けなければならなかった。

　やがて江戸時代中期になると、東北地方にも木綿が流通するようになる。大阪から瀬戸内海を経て、日本海沿岸を回り北海道へ向かう北前船の下り荷のなかでも、木綿は、塩や茶、砂糖とならぶ売れ筋商品のひとつとなった。

　けれど木綿といっても、新しい着物や反物ではなく、上方で着古された古手（古着）の着物や〈ツギ〉と呼ばれる古手木綿の端布である。着物を買えたのは資産家で、貧しい庶民には小切れを賄うのがやっとだった。〈ツギ〉を束ねた〈タバネツギ〉は米俵に詰めて運ばれ、各地の港を拠点とする古手商人や、行商の〈タベト〉を経て販売された。ひとつの俵に5、6貫（約20キロ）の布が入っていて、主婦たちはこれを5、6人で買い求め、分けあった。〈タバネツギ〉の中身は雑多で、傷みや汚れのひどいものも多く、灰汁や米のとぎ汁で洗って乾かし、ざらざらしたカワハギの皮でごみを取り除いた。

　なかでも状態の良い〈ツギ〉は〈ノシツギ〉と呼ばれ、

つなぎ合わせて着物を縫ったり、麻着物の破れやすり切れたところの継ぎあてに使用したりした。いっぽう状態の良くない〈サギ〉は、3ミリ程度の幅に切り裂いて細い紐状にし、これを緯糸に用いて「裂織」にした。この手法は、貨幣経済の遅れにより木綿が手に入りにくかった南部地方（太平洋側の旧南部藩領）で発達し、現在、私たちが耳にする「裂織」の原点となった。

　パッチワークにしても裂織にしても、現代では、有閑主婦の趣味のクラフトとして大人気であるが、もとといえば、貴重な外来資源であった木綿をいとおしむ心から生まれた手技だった。

Limited resources: cotton

Cotton raised in the milder climes of southwestern Japan is said to have been introduced to Tohoku during the Edo Period by Kitamae Merchant Marine seamen. Looking so warm and comfortable, the crewmen's cotton outfits captivated the northerners, who sadly had to go on wearing hemp because cotton wouldn't grow in the frozen north.

Came the eighteenth century, the cotton trade eventually reached Tohoku. Boats from Osaka would bear west through the Inland Sea, then double back to follow the western coast of Honshu up to Hokkaido, calling at Aomori to drop off a very saleable cargo of salt, tea and sugar – and cotton, though not fresh clean yardage or brand new kimonos.

Local landowners may have bought the occasional used kimono from Kyoto and Osaka, but all most dirt-poor Tohoku villagers could afford would be leftover scraps (*tsugi*), which Itinerant traders (*tabeto*) packed in rice bales (*tabane-tsugi*) to peddle throughout the region. Typically five or six housewives would team up to buy a single bale containing some 20-24 kgs of filthy, damaged fabric that would need to be washed in lye and rice-rinsing water, then dried and scrubbed with raspy fish skins to remove the grit and grime The best scraps (*noshi-tsugi*) they would piece together into kimono or use to patch up tattered hemp kimono; the worst scraps (*sagi*) they'd rip into narrow strips and loom them onto fixed warps to make *saki-ori* "tear-weave" fabric, a technique that Nambu District farther removed from port, where cash economy had yet to penetrate and cotton was even more difficult to obtain.

Today "patchwork" and "*saki-ori*" suggest ladies of leisure and hobby crafts, but originally these were resource-savvy ways to conserve precious imported cotton.

学生服
70 × 146 cm / 90 × 43 cm

自家製の麻布を町の仕立屋で
縫ってもらったのだろう、ミシンで
縫ってある。青森では、夏だけで
なく冬も麻服を着た。

Student uniform
70 × 146 cm / 90 × 43 cm

Machine sewing suggests this was
probably tailored in town from
homespun hemp cloth. Cold or not,
this would have been worn
year-round in Aomori.

学生服
58 × 137 cm / 81 × 45 cm

Student uniform
58 × 137 cm / 81 × 45 cm

子供服
68 × 58 cm

使い古して柔らかくなった木綿
布で手縫いした赤ん坊の肌着。
赤いビロードの紐は、女の子の
ためのものだったろうか。

Children's clothes
68 × 58 cm

Baby clothes hand-sewn out of
soft worn pieces of cotton. Was
the red velvet string for a girl?

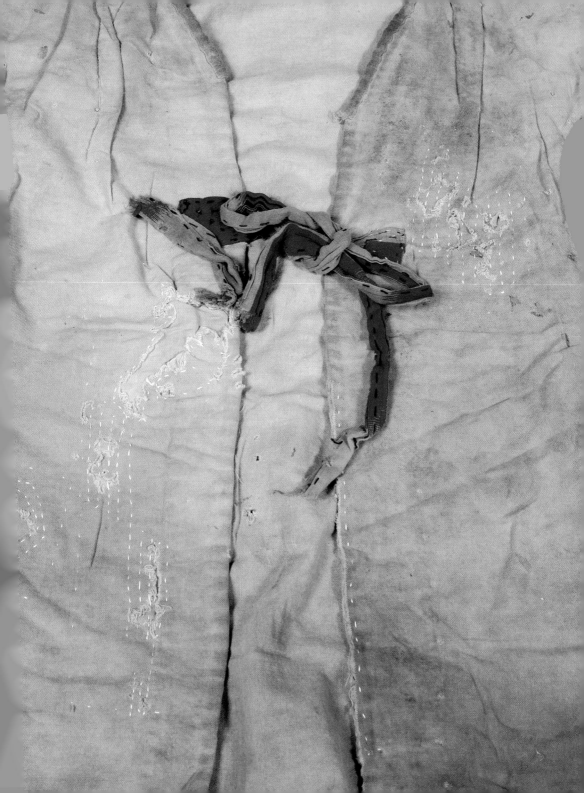

子供服
46 × 43 cm

Children's clothes
46 × 43 cm

子供服
43 × 63 cm

Children's clothes
43 × 63 cm

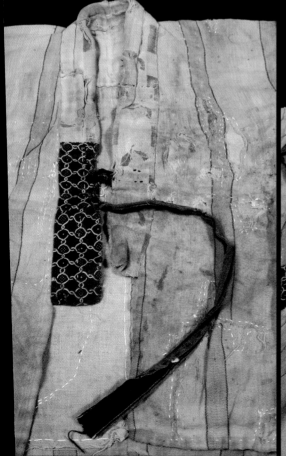

麻袋
136 × 43 cm

生成りの麻布で作った袋。

Hemp bag
136 × 43 cm

A sack made of unbleached hemp

麻袋
143 × 37 cm

紺色に染めた麻布で作った袋。
麻布を藍で染めると、虫がつき
にくいと言われた。ヒエやアワ
などの穀類を入れて保存したり、
移動する際に物入れとして使っ
た。ほころびは雑多な木綿布で
こまやかにつくろってある。

Hemp bag
143 × 37 cm

Indigo dying was said to render
hemp cloth impervious to insects,
making such bags ideal for storing
millet and other grains, as well as
for transporting valuables. Lovingly
mended with diverse cotton
fabrics.

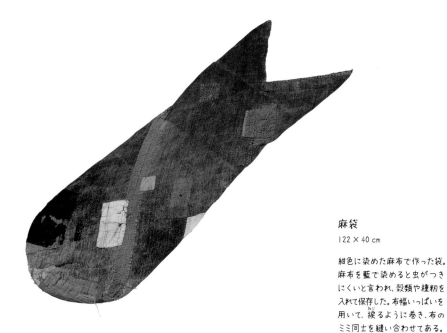

麻袋
122 × 40 cm

紺色に染めた麻布で作った袋。
麻布を藍で染めると虫がつき
にくいと言われ、穀類や種籾を
入れて保存した。布幅いっぱいを
用いて、捻（ねじ）るように巻き、布の
ミミ同士を縫い合わせてある。

Hemp bag
120 × 40 cm

Indigo dying was said to render hemp cloth impervious to insects, making such bags ideal for storing millet and seeds. Using the full width of the fabric, the pieces are sewn edge to edge.

足袋

下北半島在住の老女が亡くなっ
た後、大量の足袋が見つかった。
子供用から大人用まで、いろいろ
な大きさの足袋を家族のため
に手作りしていたのだ。足袋底
には保温と補強のために刺子
がほどこしてある。

Tabi split-toed socks

A great many *tabi* socks in
children to adult sizes were
found in the Shimokita Peninsula
home of an old woman after her
death. She had apparently made
them for her entire family. The
soles are all heavily hand-stitched
for warmth and strength.

手袋

野良仕事の際に使った手袋。物
をつかむ部分は刺子で補強した
布を縫いつけてある。

Mittens

Heavy-duty for working in the
field. The thumb grips are
reinforced with cloth patches.

腰巻
59 × 72 cm

着物の下に着る下着だったが、
おしゃれの目的もあり、祝いの席
や盆踊りの時につけて行った。
大正時代に若い女性が使った
もので、浅葱色に染めた麻布の
下に木綿の絣を組み合わせて
ある。

Koshimaki underskirt
59 × 72 cm

Worn beneath a young woman's
kimono during the Taisho Era, this
under-wrap was also intended to
be festive for dancing and other
special occasions. Pieces of cotton
ikat were added beneath light
indigo-dyed hemp cloth.

腰巻
86 × 116 cm / 58 × 77 cm

田中忠三郎さんのお祖母様が、
自分が寝込んだ時のためにと
用意していた腰巻。使い込んで
柔らかく、くたくたになった木綿
布をつなぎ合わせ、袋縫いした
もの。晒した白のグラデーション
が美しい。

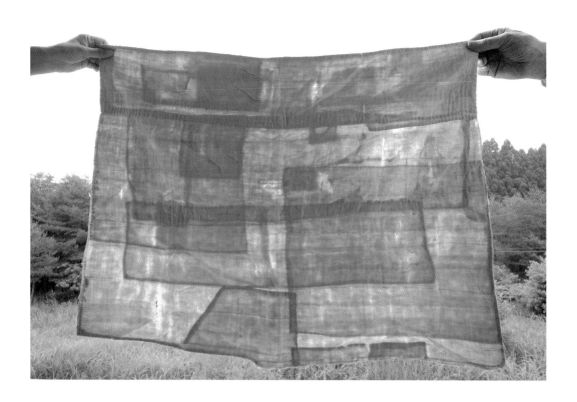

Koshimaki underskirt

86 × 116 cm / 58 × 77 cm

Chuzaburo Tanaka's grandmother readied these under-wraps for when she became bed-ridden. Pieced together with felled seams out of worn-out softened scraps of cotton, the naturally bleached gradation of white tones is lovely.

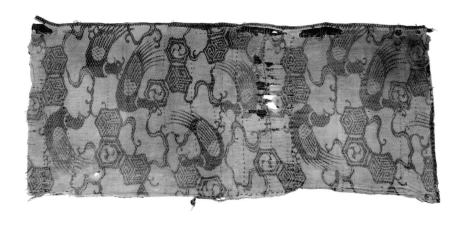

おむつ
76 × 33 cm

青森には、イジコという乳幼児
用の籠がある。籠の底に稲藁
を敷いて赤ちゃんを入れ、藁が
汚れると取り替えた。おむつは
4、5枚あれば良いほうで、使い
古して柔らかくなった布を重ね、
つなぎ合わせて作った。

Diaper
76 × 33 cm

In Aomori, *ijiko* cradles were
traditionally lined with rice straw
that was replaced whenever an
infant soiled it. Four or five
diapers pieced together out of
soft-worn fabric scraps sufficed
per child.

大人用おむつ

70 × 37 cm / 69 × 35 cm /
74 × 35 cm

田中忠三郎さんのお祖母様が、
自分が寝込んだ時のためにと
用意していたおむつ。手拭や
タオルなど、使い古して柔らかく
なった木綿布をつなぎ合わせ、
袋縫いしてある。作為のない
大胆な配置が楽しい。

Adult diapers

70 × 37 cm / 69 × 35 cm /
74 × 35 cm

Chuzaburo Tanaka's grandmother
readied these diapers for when
she became bed-ridden. Pieced
together with felled seams out of
towels and other old scraps of
cotton, the bold unintentional
composition is a delight.

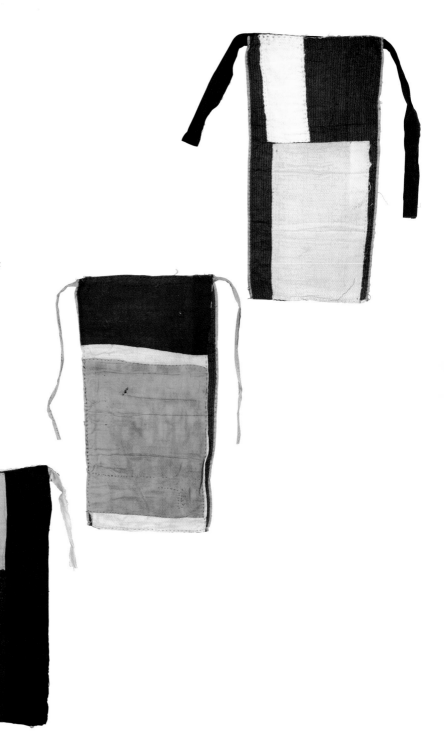

布のエコロジー

　昭和の初期まで、東北地方の農村や山村では、自給自足、地産地消があたりまえだった。地元の自然の恵みを食物とし、山野に自生する樹木や草木から繊維を取り出して衣服を手作りした人々は米粒ひとつ、布切れ1枚も粗末にしなかった。

　たとえば、新しい麻布を得るには、種蒔きから機織りまで1年がかりだった。春に種を蒔き、夏に刈り取り、晩秋に種を取る。刈り取った茎を水に浸した後、大釜で蒸して日干しにする。麻は人の背丈をはるかに越えて成長するので、一連の作業は大仕事である。

　次に茎の皮を剥ぎ、剥ぎとった皮を板の上にのせて苧引金で荒皮を削り、繊維を取り出す。この繊維をさらに細く裂いたものをつないで糸にするのが「績む」という工程だ。1反の麻布を織るには2メートルほどの麻糸を繕り結んで、5000〜6000メートルの長さにしなければならないというから、忍耐を要する仕事だった。そして、女性たちは冬の農閑期に麻布を織りあげた。ひと冬に3反織れたら上出来で、1反は自家用、1反は紺屋の染賃、1反は金に換えて、針や木綿糸、木綿布を買ったという。

　こうして手にした麻糸や麻布は貴重で、麻糸を作る過程で生じたオガラ（麻殻、皮を剥いだあとの芯）やオクズ（麻屑）も捨てずに、茅葺家屋の屋根葺きに使用したり、綿のかわりに布団に詰めたり、囲炉裏で薪と一緒に燃やして使い切った。

　田中忠三郎さんのコレクションに、お祖母様が遺された衣類がある。その中におむつがあった。赤ん坊のおむつではない。自分が老いて寝込んだ時のためにと自ら手縫いしたものだという。使い古して柔らかくなった布を縫い合わせたおむつを手にして、死を迎える老女の静かな覚悟と自分の最期を支度する精神に胸を突かれた。

　ご自分の死装束にと麻の着物も縫っておられ、忠三郎さんにこう言い聞かせたそうだ。

　　「人が死ぬと山へ行く。山道は険しく、
　　難儀な所を通るので、汗はじきの良い
　　麻の着物が良い。
　　人が死ぬと土に埋められたり、
　　焼かれて灰になったりするが、
　　麻は自分の畑で採れたものだから
　　土に還りやすい。それに比べて、
　　木綿はよそで出来たものだから、
　　土に還りにくい。」
　明治生まれの女性が実践したエコロジーだ。

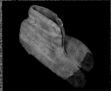

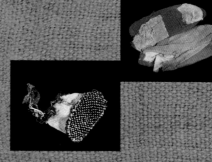

Textile ecology

Up until the early twentieth century, the villagers of Tohoku were self-sufficient, consuming only what they themselves produced. Living off the bounty of the land, scavenging the hills for wild plants whose fibers could be hand-woven, they wasted not a single grain of rice or a piece of cloth.

Making hemp cloth was a whole-year operation: planting in the spring, reaping in the summer, storing seeds in the late autumn. The harvested stems needed to be soaked, steamed and sun-dried, all very laborious efforts since hemp grows taller than human height. Next, they stripped ("retted") the stems of their outer bast, flattened them on boards and peeled away the rough outermost layer to extract the fibers, which were then split even finer and spun into thread. A one-*tan* bolt of cloth – enough for one kimono – required some five- to six-thousand meters of two-meter-long thread! A staggering amount of work in itself, but then women spent the fallow months weaving, ideally three *tan* per winter: one for the family, one to pay the indigo dyer and one to sell for money to buy needles, cotton thread and cloth.

Such hard-won hemp material was treasured; every bit of defibered stem "hurds" (*ogara*) and thread refuse (*okuzu*) was saved for thatching roofs, stuffing mattresses or burning on the hearth.

Chuzaburo Tanaka has a kimono from his grandmother in his collection. In it is a diaper – not a baby diaper, but one she sewed for when she became bed-ridden. To touch that diaper sewn from wear-softened cloth scraps is to feel the quiet resolve of an old woman preparing to die. As the old woman told Tanaka about sewing her own death robe:

"People go to the hills when they die. The mountain paths are steep and difficult to pass, you need a good hemp kimono to shed the sweat. People are buried in the ground or burned to ash when they die, but when the hemp comes from your own field, it's easy to return to the soil. By comparison, cotton from elsewhere is hard to return to the soil."

Such was the practical ecology of a woman born at the turn of last century.

ボドコ　*Bodoko*
93 × 47 cm

現代風に言えば、座布団やクッション。使い古しの木綿布を重ねてつなぎ合わせ、中に綿_{わた}がすこし入っている。冬場、お年寄りがお尻に敷いたり、腰にあてて使った。

A cushion fashioned out of layers of old cotton fabrics and small amount of cotton wadding, it was used by old people to sit on and keep their lower backs warm in winter.

ボドコ

129 × 105 cm

現代風に言えば、敷布やシーツ。2畳ほどの寝所に稲藁を敷きつめ、その上にこれを敷き、家族は一緒に眠った。洗濯するのは
年に1回。夏になると、シラミの卵を駆除するために大釜で煮沸し、川で洗った。

Bodoko
129 × 105 cm

Somewhere between a cushion and a sheet, this would have been laid on top of a two–*tatami*–mat sized—approximately 9 sq m—
floorspace strewn with straw for the whole family to sleep on. Laundered only once a year, it was boiled in a large cauldron in summer
to loosen lice nits, then washed in a river.

ボドコ

125 × 88 cm

着古した麻の着物を土台にして、麻布や木綿布を何重にも重ねて縫い合わせてある。このボドコは女性がお産する時にも使用
した。生まれてくる子供に、代々伝わる布の生命力と先祖の加護を願ったのである。

Bodoko

125 × 88 cm

This *bodoko* made from layers of hemp and cotton scraps sewed down onto a worn hemp kimono base was used during childbirth so that the newborn might be blessed with the ancestral protection and life force passed down in the fabric from generation to generation.

こたつ掛け　*Kotatsu* blanket

185 × 189 cm

こたつ掛けは、夜になると寝具にもなった。敷布にしたり、掛け布団にした。裏側は地味な木綿布だが、表側には華やかな赤い
木綿布を配し、遊び心が感じられる。

Used to cover a *kotatsu* heater-table during the day, at night it was used for bedding, either as a mattress or coverlet. The back
is plain cotton, but the front fairly shines with bright red cotton patches.

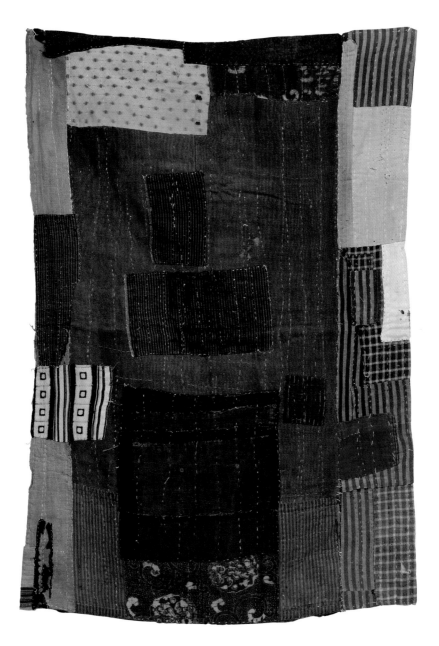

ボドコ　*Bodoko*

120 × 88 cm

2畳ほどの寝所に稲藁や枯れ草を敷きつめ、その上にボドコを敷いて寝た。敷き布団はない。ふくらみを出すために小布を詰めて
ある。上にはドンジャか、表が裂織で裏はぼろの掛け布団状のものを掛けて寝た。

*Laid on top of a two-tatami-mat size space strewn with straw, this bodoko stuffed with bits of fabric afforded little cushioning in
itself. Over top, either a donja or a some kind of quilt—larger fabric pieces face up, scruffy scraps underneath—kept the sleepers warm.*

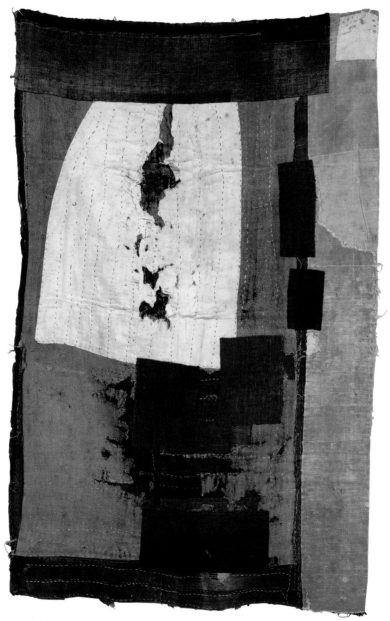

ボドコ　*Bodoko*
121 × 75 ㎝

稲藁や枯れ草の上にボドコを敷いて、家族5, 6人が一緒に寝た。冬はシラミが多く、着物を着て眠れなかったので、みな裸で
ドンジャを被って寝た。人の肌は温かく、親に抱かれて眠った子供たちは幸せだった。

A family of five or six would all sleep together on a bodoko spread out over straw. As lice tended to proliferate on kimono fabric in
winter, everyone slept naked under a donja. Skin was warmer anyway, so kids were happier sleeping in their parents arms.

布団皮　*Futon cover*

178 × 62 cm

木綿の布団皮。傷んだ部分を内側からつくろってある。

A cotton *futon* cover, every hole carefully mended from the inside.

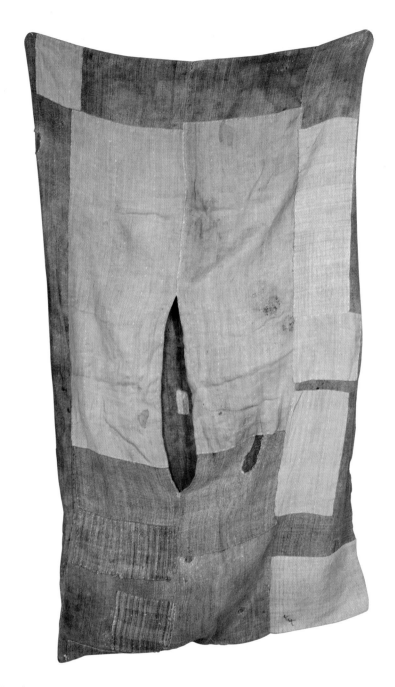

シビ布団皮
175 × 96 cm

稲藁の柔らかい葉の部分をシビといい、高価だった綿（わた）の代用品とした。自家製の麻布で作った布団皮の中にシビや、稲藁の少ない
地域では枯れ草を入れ、1年に1回交換した。傷んだ部分は古い白麻布でつくろってある。

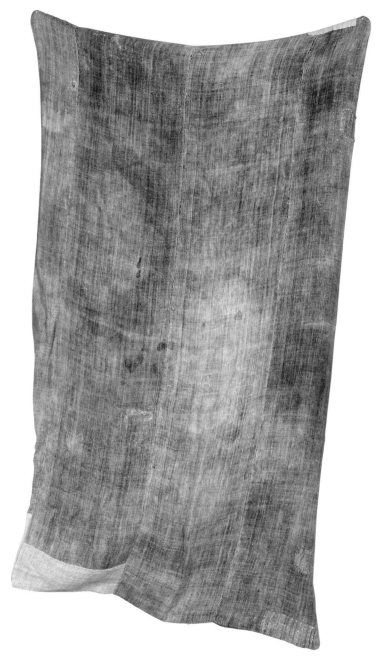

Futon cover

175 × 96 cm

Soft parts of rice straw called *shibi* were used as a substitute for expensive cotton wadding. *Shibi*, or in places with meager rice harvests, dried grass was stuffed into homespun hemp *futon* covers like this, then changed once a year. Worn spots have been repaired with old white hemp cloth.

　田中忠三郎さんのコレクションにある"ぼろ"の数々を見ていると、布を長もちさせるために尽くされた手間と膨大な時間に圧倒される。縫う人も使う人も一代ではなく、二代、三代、ときには四代にわたって、布を再生し、利用した。

　着古してすり切れた麻の着物を幾重にも重ねて、刺し縫いしたドンジャ（着物の形をした掛布団、綿のかわりに麻の屑が入っていて、ずっしり重い）。その外側を華やかな木綿裂織で包みこんだドンジャ。古くなった着物の身ごろ部分をジオメトリックにつないだ前掛けや腰巻。柔らかい木綿やメリヤス（毛織物）の小布を無数に縫い合わせた肌着。はんぱな古糸を結び、刺し綴った足袋の底……　布は何度も仕立て直され、使い回されてきた。

　これまで、これらの布類は"ぼろ"と呼ばれ、貧困の象徴として蔑まれてきた。しかし"ぼろ"を社会経済学的視点からではなく、美的な視点から見たならば、その手仕事は世界でも類を見ない素晴らしいものである。作り手が意図したものではないにせよ、限られた資源の再利用（エコロジー）、超絶技巧（テクニック）、愛情（エモーション）、経年美（パティーナ）など、きわめて今日的テーマを示唆する、テキスタイル・アートである。

　今では小説や映画を通してしか知り得ないが、昭和の前半まで、東北地方の農家の女性たちは働きどおしだった。農作業や家事を終えて、家族が寝静まった夜更けに、女性たちは機を織り、着物を縫い、つくろった。農閑期の冬には、しんしんと雪の降りつもる音を聞きながら、無心に手を動かした。その自分だけの時間に、日々の生活の辛さ、悲喜をかみしめ、心を解き放ったことだろう。そして、贅沢品ではない実用品であっても、美しいものを創る喜びは女性たちの心を弾ませたに違いない。

　北国青森の農山村で、無名の女性たちが創りだした、この希有なアートを、私たちは見くびってはならない。

　近年、欧米の目利きの間で、BOROの人気が高まっている。ニューヨークやミラノのギャラリーで展覧会が開かれ、染織美術や現代美術のコレクターがBOROを買い求めている。私たち日本人には身近すぎて、恥ずべき貧しさの名残にしか見えない粗末な布が、先入観を持たない眼には映るのだ、消費文化の対極にある希有なアートとして。

Art at odds with consumer culture

Surveying all the *boro* in Chuzaburo's Tanaka's collection, we're overwhelmed by the sheer amount of time and effort expended to make cloth last longer. Not just for one generation — two, three, sometimes even four generations reused the same fabric.

Worn-out old hemp kimono were sewn layer-on-layer to make donja, kimono-shaped bedding stuffed with impossibly heavy hemp wastage instead of cotton wadding, often with bits of colorful cotton here and there around the outside. Salvageable swatches from old kimono geometrically patched together into aprons and koshimaki petticoats. Countless bits of soft cotton and *meriyasu* woolens pieced into undergarments. Odd lengths of old thread tied end-to-end and stitched firmly into the soles of tabi footwear… every scrap was reused over and over again.

Up to now, people have reviled *boro* as the very embodiment of poverty. If, however, we look at the aesthetics of boro instead of the socio-economics, we may see an incomparable degree of wonderful handiwork. The creators' intentions aside, in terms of ecological awareness, technique, emotion and patina, these are extremely evocative contemporary works of textile art.

Tohoku farmwomen of the early twentieth century were incredibly hard workers, the stuff of novels and movies. After finishing the farmwork and household chores, after the rest of the family had gone to sleep, the womenfolk would stay up weaving on their looms, sewing and mending kimono. During the fallow winter months, as the snow piled high, they ceaselessly busied their hands. Such solitary moments were probably the only chance they had to chew on the hardships, joys and sorrows of daily life. No luxuries to be had, still they could find some uplifting release by creating beauty in practical things.

We cannot help but be humbled by these rare works of art fashioned by nameless women from the northlands of Aomori. In recent years, boro aesthetics have come to the attention of connoisseurs in the West. At exhibitions in New York and Milano, textile and contemporary art collectors are buying *boro*, while we Japanese are still too close, too ashamed of these roughshod reminders of our not-so-distant impoverished past. Only once we view these fabric artworks with unprejudiced eyes we will see them as anything-but-crude, brilliant antitheses to rampant consumerism.

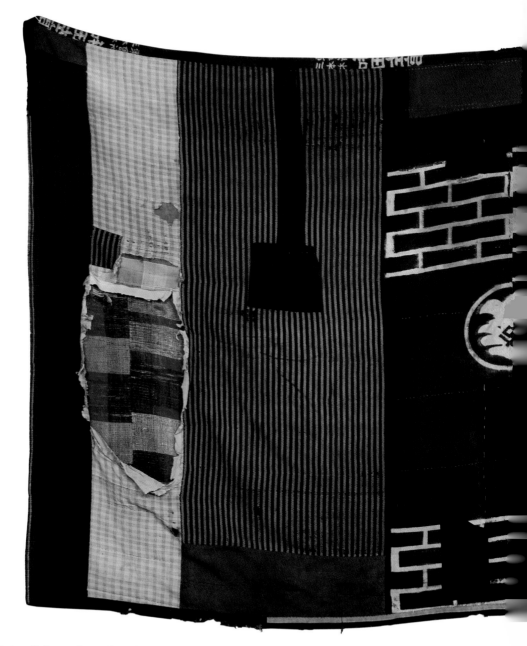

こたつ掛け　*Kotatsu* blanket
144 × 167 cm

着古した刺子の着物や商家の半纏などをつないで作ったこたつ掛け。中に古くなった裂織のこたつ掛けを入れ、こたつの中の温かい
空気が逃げないように重くしてある。冬は、夜になるとこれを掛けて眠った。

A kotatsu heater-table blanket patched together out of an old sashiko-stitched kimono and a merchant's short hanten jacket.
Stuffed with old fabric scraps to make it heavier and keep the heated air from escaping, on winter nights it was also used for a coverlet.

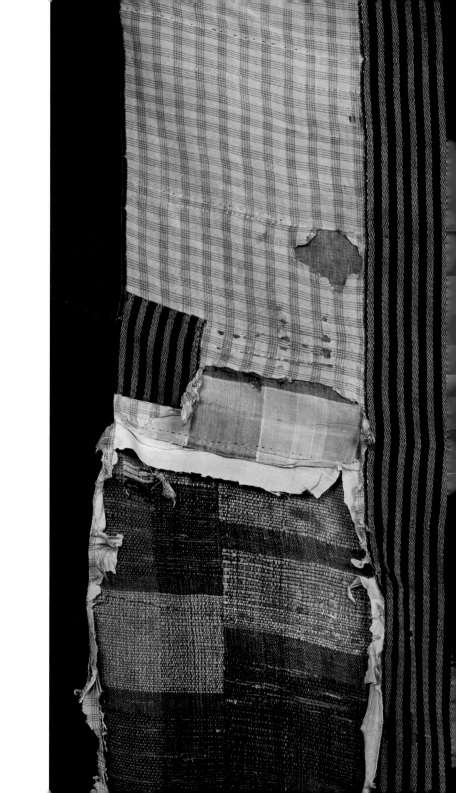

こたつ掛け
185 × 189 cm

麻や木綿の雑多な古布を再利
用して作ったこたつ掛けは、夜に
なると掛け布団になった。傷んだ
表面が過酷な使用を物語り、
その下からのぞく布の層が年月
の経過と手仕事の積み重ねを
証している。

Kotatsu blanket
185 × 196 cm

This *kotatsu* heater-table cover
recombines many different pieces
of hemp and cotton cloth, and
was used as a coverlet at night.
The scarred surface attest to
heavy use, while the many layers
visible underneath evidence long
years of hand-stitching and
mending.

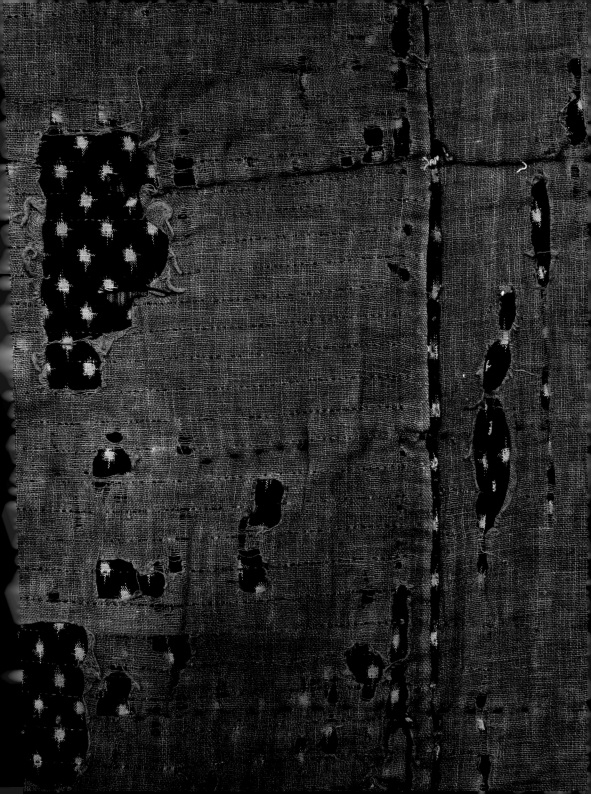

モノには人の心が投影される

　青森の農村や山村の人々は、着物を何枚持っていた
だろう。仕事着一式と家で着る着物を持っていれば、
多いほうだったかもしれない。文字通り、着た切り雀
の人もいただろう。けれどこれらの"ぼろ"には、こん
なものを着ていた人は、貧しくても、満ち足りていた
に違いない、と思わせる存在感がある。

　青森のぼろほどみごとなぼろはない。寒冷地の青森
では綿花が育たず、とくに木綿の入手が困難だった農
山村部では昭和初期まで麻布の生活が続いた歴史
的背景があり、過酷な気候風土や生活の困窮に反比
例して、女性たちの家族への思い、布へのいつくしみ
が深く、ぼろに蓄積された手仕事と感情の度合いが
圧倒的だからだ。

　世界に類のない衣文化が生まれた背景には、人生を
受け入れ、人と物をいつくしみながら、命を全うする
生き方があった。

　この本を作りながら、20世紀の偉大なファッション・
デザイナー、ココ・シャネルのことを思い出した。1971年
にシャネルが亡くなったとき、ホテル・リッツの部屋の
クローゼットに遺されていたのは、スーツが2着だけ
だったという。仕事一筋のシャネルにとって、なにより
大事なのは仕事着だったのだろう。イブニングドレス
などなくても、これさえあれば生きてゆける、2着の
スーツを手直しして愛用していたのだ。

　数をたくさん持つことや、高価な物を持つことが豊
かさではない。自分に大切なことを知り、必要な物を
持てることが豊かさだ。そんなことを青森のぼろから
教わった。

　ご紹介したぼろは、青森出身の民俗学研究家・田中
忠三郎さんのコレクションで、40年にわたるフィール
ドワークの成果である。若いころ、縄文遺跡の発掘に
夢中になった田中さんは、縄文時代の人々の衣食住を
知りたいという思いから、青森の僻村を訪ねて聞き取り
調査を行ない、生活用具を収集した。

　田中コレクションには、重要有形民俗文化財に指定
されている津軽こぎん刺しや南部菱刺しの着物類も
あるが、これらの工芸的価値の高い着物に比べると、
世間ではぼろへの関心は皆無で、田中さんの他にぼろ
を集める人はいなかった。田中さんが集めていなかっ
たら、大半は棄てられていただろう。田中さんの先見の
明と地道な収集のおかげで、私たちはこの文化遺産に
触れることができることを心から感謝したい。

Matter reflects mind

How many kimono did Aomori fisherfolk and farmers own? Very likely they wore the same one kimono at all times, with not even separate work clothes. And yet, however poor, we may discern a certain sense of fulfillment in these boro articles.

There's no *boro* so perfectly worn as Aomori *boro*. Considering the historical fact that villagers in Aomori, where cotton doesn' t grow and is difficult to come by, lived their entire lives in hemp cloth (at least until the early Showa Era), the bitterness of the climate and hardship of their lives was matched only by the local women's loving concern for their families and fondness for the fabric itself, as evidenced by the overwhelming intensity of hand-crafting and passion concentrated in their *boro* creations. Behind this unparalleled textile culture was a way of life that fully accepted this human existence and, endearing both people and things, sought of make the best of their energies.

In doing this book, I was reminded of Coco Chanel, one of the greats of twentieth century fashion design who, when she died in 1971, left only two suits hanging in her wardrobe at the Hotel Ritz. Throughout her lifelong career, these work clothes were probably her most important possessions. No evening dress, nothing fancy – just two suits she would alter as needed, that was enough to get by.

Having lots of expensive things is not wealth. Knowing what's really important and necessary for oneself, that's real wealth. That's what this Aomori boro teaches us.

The boro presented herein is the sum of 40 years of fieldwork by Aomori's own ethnographic researcher Chuzaburo Tanaka. An archeology enthusiast in his youth, his desire to learn more about how the prehistoric Jomon people dressed, ate and dwelled drove him to remote villages to survey local lore and collect daily life implements.

There are, of course, examples of designated Important Cultural Property *kogin-sashi* and *hishi-zashi* stitched kimono and other highly acclaimed craftworks in Tanaka's collection, though by contrast no one else has shown the least interest in *boro*. If Tanaka had not collected them, most would have been cast off, lost or destroyed. It's only thanks to his foresight and persistent selfless efforts we have any access to this very cultural heritage.

謝辞

『サキオリから裂織へ』(田中忠三郎著)と題された、1冊のカタログに出会ったことが、本書を作るきっかけになった。

　田中忠三郎さんは1933年、青森県下北郡(現むつ市)川内町に生まれた。小学校6年生で終戦を迎え、翌年弘前の中学校に入学。下宿生活の寂しさから散歩に通った弘前公園で拾った石と瓶(かめ)のカケラが、図書館にあった『日本考古学概要』という本に写真入りで紹介されていたことに感激、いっぺんに少年考古学マニアになった。

　学校を終えて家業の水産加工業を手伝いながら近場での発掘に精を出すが、仕事のほうがおろそかになって実家にいたたまれなくなり、23歳で家を出る。故郷の川内町と陸奥湾を隔てた対岸にある、東津軽郡平内町で金物屋の住み込み運転手となり、昼は金物屋で働きながら、夜になると懐中電灯の明かりで町内の遺跡発掘という生活。開田事業や道路拡張工事で破壊寸前の遺跡を調査するために、その1年後からは仕事も辞めて発掘に人生を賭けるようになった。

　「そんな発掘生活を私は10年続けた。友人はよく"どうやって暮らしていた?"と問うが、私は笑って答えない。惨めで悲しく、孤独と飢えと寒さとの戦いだったからである」と田中さんは自著で記している(『下北 忘れえぬ人びと』荒蝦夷刊)。孤独な10年間の発掘生活のあと、平内町教育委員会に文化財担当として勤務するようになり、その後小川原湖民俗博物館に移るが、そのころから田中さんの興味は考古学から民俗・民具の世界へと移っていった。

原始時代、人間は毛皮を纏っていたと一般的に考えられているが、冬はともかく夏に毛皮では暑すぎるし、また「素晴らしい紋様の土器を見ると、これほど造形感覚の鋭い人々が、粗末な毛皮を纏うはずがない、美しい衣で身を飾っていたと思った」ことから、身近な姥や古老から昔の衣の話を聞こうと訪ね歩く、田中さんの新たなフィールドワークが始まる。昭和40年代のことだった。

「そのことでずいぶんと長い間、痛烈な批判と冷笑を浴びた。"ボロやがらくたを収集、調査している"と」と田中さんは書いているが、足かけ40年間にわたる収集生活で、衣・食・住にかかわる衣服や民具が2万点あまりという膨大なコレクションとなり、そのうち刺し子着786点が国の有形民俗文化財に、紡績用具520点が県の有形民俗文化財に指定されることになった。1975年には寺山修司の『田園に死す』、1990年には黒澤明監督晩年の作品となった『夢』に衣装を提供している。

今年75歳になった田中忠三郎さんは、病を抱えながら、いまでも毎日のように青森市郊外にある巨大な倉庫に通い、コレクションの整理に没頭している。手伝う者も、引き継ごうという者もいないまま。刺し子のように民芸としてすでに評価が確立しているものは、文化財に指定されたが、田中さんがもっとも愛するぼろについては、いまだに評価の対象外、県内に展示する施設ひとつない状態である。冒頭にあげたカタログも、写真のプロではない田中さんが自分ひとりで撮影し、原稿を書き、県内の印刷所に発注した自費出版物なのだ。本書に収録したのは、すべて田中さんのコレクションを、あらためて撮影させていただいたものである。

地元青森での評価はともかくとして、ぼろ＝BOROはいまやアート、テキスタイル・デザインの分野では共通語となるほど、世界的な評価の気運が高まっている。日本でも東北にかぎらず、全国にひろがる農漁民のぼろを精力的に発掘する人々が増えてきた。ただ、南方のぼろが木綿を主体としたものであるのに対し、本書で紹介する青森のぼろは、あくまでも麻を主材料とするものだ。麻は木綿ほどの温かさを持たないから、必然的に重ねる枚数が多くなり、厚くなる。皮肉なことに、厳しく貧しい環境が、特異な重層の美を生む原動力となったのだ。

だれにも理解されないまま、たったひとり山から村へ、浜からまた山へと40年間にわたって収集の旅を続けてきた田中忠三郎さんの成果がなかったら、この本は生まれなかったし、僕らがぼろの魅力を知ることもなかったろう。

南方熊楠や宮本常一の例を引くまでもなく、日本の民俗学の業績の多くは、在野の研究者によってもたらされてきた。"ぼろ"という奇跡的なテキスタイル・アートとともに、またひとり、北の国の片隅で黙々とフィールドワークを続ける在野の偉人を生んでくれたことを、僕らは青森の地に深く感謝したい。

Acknowledgements

This book would not exist had we not happened upon a monograph entitled *From Rags to Saki-Ori* by Chuzaburo Tanaka.

Born in 1933 in Kawanai, a small town in Aomori Prefecture, Tanaka was a sixth-grade student when World War II ended. Moving to Hirosaki City from the next year to attend middle school, he was surprised to see ancient rocks and shards found in the very same Hirosaki Park where he sometimes strolled pictured in a library book and immediately became fascinated by archeology.

After graduating, he helped out with the family seafood business, but was clearly more interested in local digs, and eventually left home at 23. He found work in a nearby Hiranaicho as a driver and shop clerk in a hardware store, but at nights he would still go digging by flashlight. Only a year later, however, he quit his job in order to survey ancient sites before they were destroyed by clearing farmland and building roads.

Writes Tanaka in his memoirs, "I was a digger for ten years. Friends asked, 'How do you make a living?' but I'd just laugh. It was one long, miserable fight against loneliness and hunger and cold." Finally, after ten years of solitary digging, he became Cultural Property Liaison of the Hiranai Board of Education, then later went on he a post at the Ogawara Ethnology Museum, whereupon his interest shifted from archeology to ethnography and the realm of folk implements.

The ancient proto-Japanese are generally imagined in animal skins, at least in winter, though obviously too hot for summer. But as Tanaka recalls, "When I looked at the wonderful patterns on ancient earthenwares, I knew that people with such a keen decorative sense would not just wrap up in furs – they must have dressed up in more attractive weavings." And so, from around 1965, he embarked on new fieldwork, gathering oral lore from elders about clothing "in the old days."

"For a long time, I was subjected to intense criticism and ridicule for 'picking rags and junk'," writes Tanaka, but four decades on he had amassed an enormous collection of some twenty thousand folk items related to the food, clothing and shelter, to the very life of the people. Among these, 786 pieces of *sashiko*-stitched clothing have been designated National Cultural Properties and 520 spinning and weaving tools are now Prefectural Cultural Properties. In 1975, Tanaka provided costumes for the Shuji Terayama film *Den'en ni Sisu* (Death in the Country) and again in 1990 for the Akira Kurosawa film *Dreams*.

Now 75 and in ill health, Chuzaburo Tanaka still commutes every day to a huge warehouse on the outskirts of Aomori City in an on-going effort to catalog his vast collection. All without any helper or anyone to succeed him. Meanwhile his favorite *boro* pieces still elude recognition; no institution public or private will deign to even exhibit them. The monograph mentioned at the beginning was photographed, published and paid for entirely by himself (we have since re-photographed Mr. Tanaka's collection for this present edition.)

Despite disfavor in Aomori, the "rag" aesthetic is gaining worldwide acclaim in both art and textile design. All over Japan, more and more people are actively digging up their local boro roots, the only difference being that further south the rags are mostly cotton, whereas these ones from Aomori are almost exclusively hemp. And because hemp is not nearly as warm as cotton, the layering is necessarily thicker – hence that much more complex. Ironically, the poorer and harsher the setting, the stronger the urge to create overlays of incredible beauty.

Without the thankless efforts of Chuzaburo Tanaka who traipsed over mountain and rugged seacoast for forty years collecting these pieces, we would never have known the beauty of boro. Major ethnological discoveries both in Japan and elsewhere have been made by persons outside the field proper. We offer our heartfelt gratitude to Aomori for giving us this lone eccentric who, like the miraculous textile art of boro itself, silently persevered in the frozen north.

BORO

つぎ、はぎ、いかす。青森のぼろ布文化
Rags and Tatters from the Far North of Japan

2009年1月7日　第1版 第1刷発行
2011年9月7日　第1版 第2刷発行
編集：小出由紀子・都築響一
撮影：都築響一
（120,121ページ撮影・田中忠三郎）

ブックデザイン：青木康子
翻訳：アルフレッド・バーンバウム

モデル：下池初栄・桝井昌也・水野響
協力：田中忠三郎コレクション
参考資料：田中忠三郎『サキオリから裂織へ』
（連絡先：〒030-0944 青森市筒井字八ッ橋203-2）

発行人　高比良公成
発行所　株式会社アスペクト
〒101-0054東京都千代田区神田錦町3-18-3 錦三ビル3F
電話03-5281-2551　FAX03-5281-2552
ホームページ http://www.aspect.co.jp

印刷所　光村印刷株式会社

BORO

Rags and Tatters from the Far North of Japan

Edited by Yukiko Koide and Kyoichi Tsuzuki
Photographed by Kyoichi Tsuzuki
(except page120,121 by Chuzaburo Tanaka)
Designed by Yasuko Aoki
Translated by Alfred Birnbaum

Models: Hatsue Simoike, Masaya Masui, Hibiki Mizuno

Special thanks to Chuzaburo Tanaka Collection

First Published in Japan 2008 by ASPECT Corp.
Kinsan Bldg.3F 3-18-3 KandaNishikicho Chiyoda-ku
Tokyo, Japan ZIP101-0054
TEL+81-3-5281-2551/FAX+81-3-5281-2552
Homepage/http://www.aspect.co.jp
E-mail/info@aspect.co.jp